Found

from *Detective Dinosaur:*
Lost and Found

by James Skofield
illustrated by R.W. Alley

HOUGHTON MIFFLIN   BOSTON

One night Detective Dinosaur and
Officer Pterodactyl heard a strange
sound. It came from the garage.
Slowly they opened the garage door.

They a saw a brown paper bag.
It was moving!
"Is it an alligator?" asked
Detective Dinosaur.

4

"It is too small to be an alligator, sir,"
said Officer Pterodactyl.

"Meow," said the paper bag.

Detective Dinosaur jumped.

"A snake!" he cried.

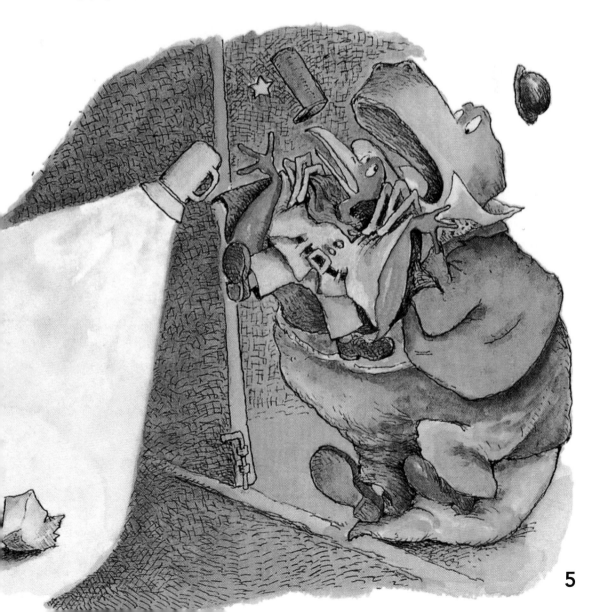

"I do not think so, sir,"
said Officer Perodactyl. She
reached into the paper bag
and pulled out a kitten.

"What is a kitten doing here?"
asked Detective Dinosaur.

"I think she is lost, sir,"
said Officer Pterodactyl.

They gave the kitten some milk.
Then the kitten went to sleep.

The next day they put up signs:

HAVE YOU LOST THIS KITTEN?
CALL THE POLICE STATION.

They waited days and weeks
and months, but no one called.

"Poor lost kitty," said
Detective Dinosaur.

One evening Chief Tyrannosaurus
could not find his keys.

Everybody looked for them.
They looked in lockers.
They looked under desks.
   "Where are my keys?"
yelled Chief Tyrannosaurus.

Just then the kitten dragged
the keys into the room.

"Well done, kitty!" said the Chief.
"What is your name?"

"She does not have a name,
Chief," said Detective Dinosaur.
"She is a lost kitty."

"Nonsense," said the Chief.
"She is a found kitty. She
found my keys! I will call her
Cadet Kitty."

Cadet Kitty purred loudly.

"I guess she isn't a poor lost kitty after all," said Detective Dinosaur. "We found her."

"Or," said Officer Pterodactyl, "maybe she found us."

CASE CLOSED